1 TABLE OF CONTENTS

Preparation and restraint are critical for safely and effectively pressure washing your home's exterior but the results are worth it.

A pressure washer turns the flow from a regular garden hose into a powerful spray. Whether prepping for a fresh coat of paint or simply washing away built-up dirt and grime, learning how to use a pressure washer can be a skill to tackle various surfaces and projects around your home's exterior. But it can also easily cause surface damage if not used correctly, so preparation and restraint are key. Here's what you need to know to effectively and safely

freshen up common exterior surfaces using a pressure washer.

Safety Note

Never power-wash a surface with lead paint. If it's possible the surface you're cleaning was painted before 1978, you should have it tested before beginning any work.

2.1 WHAT YOU'LL NEED

Equipment / Tools

- Broom

- Pressure washer (gas or electric)

- Pressure washer extensions (optional)

- Hose

- Safety glasses

- Closed-toed shoes

- Materials

- Tarp or heavy duty plastic

- Duct tape

- Cleaning solutions

- Extra fuel (gas powered only)

Instructions

Before You Begin: How to Choose a Pressure Washer

There are two types of pressure washers: gas and electric. They're rated for residential or commercial use, and the main characteristics for picking a model are the PSI (pounds per square inch) and GPM (gallons per minute). "The higher the PSI, the more power to blast the dirt from the surfaces, and the higher the GPM, the faster you can clean the large.

What you need depends on the project and surface you're tackling. More delicate surfaces require less pressure, and a simple rinse versus tackling stuck-on muck can also impact the oomph needed behind the spray. According to RYOBI, residential-rated gas machines with 2,600-3,400 PSI and 2.3-2.6 GPM are ideal for tackling various larger home exterior projects.

2.2 THE 8 BEST PRESSURE WASHERS FOR EVERY OUTDOOR CLEANING JOB

Water pressure is not a cure-all; you risk damaging a surface by assuming a stronger force or lingering on one spot will remove stains, mildew, or gunk. "Soap can help to break things down better. "For example, you would want to use an oil degreaser for stains on your driveway since just water by itself won't cut it."

Cleaning solutions can be applied with or without the pressure washer. Alternatives like spray guns, hose attachments, or a sponge or roller method can also get the job done, but pressure washers are especially helpful for something like siding, where added force moves soap into hard-to-reach places.

When applied with a pressure washer, detergent gets incorporated through a soap tank on the machine or a pressure washer siphon tube placed in an external cleaning solution. It's important to know what kind of solution you'll use and how it gets used with the device. There are many pressure-washer-approved cleaning products specific to the surface (such as concrete and driveway detergents) or the problem you're tackling (such as rust-fighting solutions.)

2.3 HOW TO CLEAN A CONCRETE PATIO TO REMOVE TOUGH STAINS

How to Use a Pressure Washer

Prepare Area

Start by relocating items like potted plants, patio furniture, and other accessories from the area to be cleaned. Sweep away large debris like rocks and twigs that could become projectiles when sprayed. Cover nearby plants and landscaping with a tarp, and cover outdoor lights, sound systems, or other features if they're in the direct path of water or could receive significant spray.

House and garage exteriors require additional consideration. Close windows and doors, and cover outlets, doorbells, light fixtures, and air conditioning units with tarps or plastic and duct tape if possible. Shut off the electricity to exterior outlets on the section you're pressure washing. The goal is to avoid water getting inside your home and prevent water and electricity from mixing.

If the area has cracks or gaps, like missing mortar or dents in fencing, consider patching them before pressure washing. This will protect its structural integrity and prevent water from getting behind a protective exterior covering.

Assemble Pressure Washer and Accessories

Follow the manufacturer's instructions for assembling the pressure washer. Attach any extension or telescoping wands you want to use; these are popular accessories for cleaning higher, harder-to-reach siding. For gas-powered models, be sure to add fuel and lubricant as directed.

Find a hose (ensure there are no leaks!) that will connect the pressure washer to your home's water supply. If using a cleaning solution, gather plenty of detergent and any related gear needed to apply it. Use safety glasses and closed-toed shoes to protect yourself from splashback, ricocheting debris, or accidentally sweeping the powerful steam of water across your toes.

Having extra fuel and oil available for gas models can also save you from having to stop mid-project (and prevent damage to the machine).

Select the Right Nozzles

Pressure washers come with multiple nozzles (though some machines have an adjustable nozzle with various spray settings), controlling how the water comes from the pressure washer. Nozzles are generally universal in color and degree, and machines might come with some or all of the ones listed here:

- 0-degree spray (red): The most powerful spray, this is rarely used and not recommended for general home exterior cleaning projects.

- 15-degree spray (yellow): Good for hard surfaces and tough jobs like stripping paint
- 25-degree spray (green): Good for concrete and hard, unpainted siding
- 40-degree spray (white): Good for softer surfaces prone to damage and most sidings
- Low-pressure soap/detergent nozzle (color varies): Used to apply cleaning solution

Nozzles with smaller degrees offer a stronger, more direct spray; larger degrees have a wider, less concentrated force, making them safer on more surfaces. Home exterior projects generally use a low-pressure detergent nozzle and a 25- or 40-degree spray.

While it's safe to pressure wash many surfaces, some materials, like fiber cement siding, are not typically recommended to be cleaned with a pressure washer. It's also wise to avoid pressure washing painted surfaces and fragile surfaces like old brick, wood, or stucco. Do some research on the material you intend to clean before getting started. Pressure washer user manuals usually have nozzle guidance, and when possible, consult the surface manufacturer for information about the material. Always err on the side of caution.

Connect Hose

Connect a regular garden hose to your home's water supply, and run it for 30-60 seconds to eliminate air and any trapped materials. Turn off the spigot, then connect the other end of the hose to the water intake on the pressure washer.

Consistent pressure from your home's water source is needed to keep the washer working smoothly. Use a water pressure gauge attached to the spigot to test your source's performance. If it measures between 40 and 60 PSI, the device should work fine.

Test Pressure Washer

If you aren't wearing it already, it's a good time to put on your safety gear. Next, put a low-pressure nozzle onto the end of the pressure washer wand; it should easily click into place. Turn on the water supply by fully opening the spigot. Aiming in a safe direction, release the pressure washer trigger lock and press the trigger to purge air from the setup, leaving it on until water comes from the wand.

Now you are ready to turn on the pressure washer. For most electric models, it's as simple as an off-on switch, while gas-powered machines use a fuel valve, choke, and starter. But don't turn on the pressure washer until you're ready to get started; it's bad for the machine to run too long without being used.

Apply Detergent (If Applicable)

Prepare and apply the cleaning solution according to the manufacturer's instructions. If using the pressure washer to apply the detergent, make sure you're incorporating it (into the machine tank or through the siphon tube) as directed and that the low-pressure soap nozzle is in place.

For vertical surfaces like siding, fences, sloped driveways, or landscaping steps, apply the cleaning solution from bottom to top, sweeping from side to side so soap runs downward and keeps the below areas wet. Manufacturer instructions will have advice on how long to let the detergent sit before washing.

Clean with Pressure Washer

Turn on the machine. Unlock and engage the trigger to activate the pressure washer, choosing a small area first to test the pressure. For something like siding, start with the nozzle at least four feet away from the surface to not apply too much pressure immediately. Aim the spray farther in front of you for decking or horizontal surfaces, not directly down. Walk closer and adjust the angle you're holding the wand until the surface gets clean but isn't damaged. Don't get too close to the surface with the nozzle.

If the current setup isn't doing the trick, you can try switching the nozzle, being cautious to start at a distance again. Nozzle tips shouldn't be changed unless the engine is turned off, the pressure has been relieved from the wand, and the trigger lock is engaged.

Once you've found the right position, get cleaning. Spray away from yourself, especially with horizontal surfaces. For vertical surfaces, start at the top of the section you're working on, sweeping back and forth while moving down so that dirt and debris fall into areas waiting to be cleaned. For even cleaning, use overlapping strokes, and don't linger with direct pressure on one spot. Avoid directly spraying what you've covered, like outlets, light fixtures, and areas that can let water into the home, such as doors and windows. Don't use the pressure washer around meters, satellites, cable boxes, power lines, or other utilities.

Repeat, Rinse, and Store

Repeat the soaping and washing as necessary if you've split your project into sections. Then, rinse any residue with the lower-pressure soap nozzle or a hose attached to your home's water supply.

When finished with the pressure washer, turn off the machine and engage the trigger safety lock. Next, turn off the water source. Undo the lock and engage the wand to release any remaining water and pressure from the nozzle. Follow manufacturer instructions for storing the machine.

2.4 More Pressure-Washing Tips for Success

Start with Hard Surfaces: If you're nervous about power washing for the first time, choose a sturdy surface. "A good first project would be the driveway/sidewalk since it is the least likely to get damaged.

Divide and Conquer: Break large projects into sections that you can manage in a timely manner. You don't want to run out of fuel at an inconvenient time, or soap to dry before you can pressure wash it.

Utilize Pressure Washer Accessories: In addition to specific cleaning solutions, look for accessories related to the project. "There are tons of accessories to make each job easier and faster. "For example, if cleaning a driveway, a surface cleaner will drastically reduce the time needed to finish the project."

Consider Renting: Pressure washers are available for rent from home improvement stores, which provide an opportunity to talk with a pro who can help choose the best machine and accessories for your job.

Check the Weather: Avoid pressure washing during high temperatures and in direct sunlight. "Choose a day with mild weather where the sun won't be too intense to the point that your detergents dry before having the chance to rinse them off.

2.5 GAS VS. ELECTRIC PRESSURE WASHERS: WHAT'S THE DIFFERENCE?

Pressure washers are popular home maintenance tools used to clean decks, patio stones, and driveways. Used on a low setting and with the appropriate technique, pressure washers are also excellent for cleaning fences, siding, and even vehicles.

Pressure washers are available as gas or electric tools, but before deciding which type is suited for your home, it's recommended to learn more about the differences between gas and electric pressure washers. Use this guide to break down the pros and cons of gas and electric pressure washers so you can figure out the best option for your project.

6 Things to Consider When Choosing a Gas or Electric Pressure Washer

Power

One of the main factors to consider is the power output of the pressure washer. This is typically measured in two ways: The flow rate, measured in gallons per minute (GPM), is the amount of water the pressure washer releases, while the output pressure is measured in pounds per square inch (PSI). High-power tools can be used to scrub cement, concrete, and asphalt, though the high pressure can damage the target surface if the pressure washer is not properly directed and controlled.

Electric pressure washers are generally seen as light-duty power tools because they do not generate the same amount of power as a gas pressure washer. On average, the power output of an electric pressure washer will produce about 1.5 to 2.5 GPM at a water pressure that ranges from 1,500 to 3,000 PSI. Gas pressure washers range from 2,500 to more than 4,000 PSI and typically have a flow rate between 2.5 to 4 GPM.

If the pressure is too high, the water spraying out of a pressure washer could damage the target surface. Depending on the type of pressure washer and the max psi of the unit, a pressure washer could even chip patio stones. For this reason, it's important to use pressure washers with appropriate skill and caution.

Safety

Safety should always be a primary consideration when working with any type of power tool. Pressure washers are no exception. The powerful spray of water produced by these tools is enough to bruise or break skin and can cause permanent damage to sensitive areas of the body, like the eyes or ears.

Given that gas pressure washers tend to have a higher power output than electric pressure washers, a gas model presents a higher risk of injury than an electric model. However, electric pressure washers can still cause physical harm and should not be handled carelessly. These light-duty products have a power cord that can create a tripping hazard. Additionally, the motor on both electric and gas pressure washers can get hot during use, so it's a good idea to keep your hands, arms, and any exposed skin away from the motor and exhaust ports.

Maintenance

It can be easy to overlook the fact that even tools that are commonly used for cleaning require regular maintenance. Electric pressure washers are lighter and typically easier to maintain than gas pressure washers, but even these garden tools need semi-regular lubrication to keep the pump operating properly. Electric pressure washers should also be cleaned after every use.

Gas pressure washers have combustion engines with oil and gas filters that need to be changed about once per year. It's also necessary to change the oil in the pressure washer when needed and to replace the spark plug if it fails to ensure that the pressure washer will start without an issue. Beyond these infrequent maintenance tasks, you also need to keep the pump lubricated and clean the gas pressure washer after each use.

Environmental Impact

Before purchasing a new power tool, it's a good idea to look into the ecological cost of buying and using one of these machines. This should include the waste, noise pollution, emissions, and any other impacts the tool has on the local environment.

Electric pressure washers are the better option for low environmental impact. They run at about 80 decibels (dB), which is around the same level as a standard vacuum cleaner. These tools use clean electricity for power, so they don't produce emissions or rely on fossil fuels for operations.

Gas pressure washers are made for power, not environmental protection. They can operate at a volume of more than 100 dB. For reference, hearing protection is recommended when continuous noise levels exceed 85 dB, which is why it's important to make sure to have earplugs when working with this tool. The gas and oil used to operate the pressure washer are non-renewable resources that produce harmful emissions, so if you are looking for an eco-friendly tool, the electric model is a better choice.

Ease of Use

The way in which a pressure washer operates should be factored into your considerations before choosing between gas vs. electric pressure washers. Gas pressure washers are more powerful and easier to use for heavy-duty cleaning. You won't have to worry about tripping over a power cord as you work, but gas pressure washers are loud and produce harmful emissions, so they should only be used outdoors.

Electric pressure washers are lighter and easier to move around than gas models. However, you need to run a power cord to the unit for the pressure washer to function, which can create a tripping hazard. As long as you don't mind watching your step around the power cord, electric pressure washers are suitable for both indoor and outdoor use, making them a good option for light cleaning in the garage, barn, or shed.

Cost

While the price of a product relies heavily on the manufacturer, in most cases, there is a significant difference between the cost of an electric pressure washer and the cost of a gas pressure washer. Gas pressure washers tend to be more expensive than electric units, with an average price ranging from $300 to $600. Electric pressure washers fall well below this range, at an average price of $100 to $400.

After the initial purchase, electric pressure washers are powered by electricity from the home, while gas pressure washers require fuel and oil to function. Generally, the cost of electricity is slightly higher than the cost of gas and oil, though the difference in operating costs is relatively little.

There is a wide range of factors to consider before deciding between a gas or electric pressure washer, including power, safety factors, maintenance requirements, ease of use, environmental impact, and cost. Take some time to weigh the benefits and drawbacks of each while you consider your needs to find the best type of pressure washer for your home.

More powerful than comparable electric units Suited for light-duty work

Louder and relies on gasoline for power Quiet and eco-friendly operation

Convenient cordless operation Require less maintenance than gas units

Powerful spray can be a safety hazard Lower power operation presents less personal risk

High durability More affordable

3 YOUR 9-STEP GUIDE TO STARTING A PRESSURE WASHING BUSINESS FROM SCRATCH

Starting a pressure washing business is a smart idea that can help you set your own schedule, do satisfying work, and make good money doing it.

It's important to start your business on the right foot and set yourself up for long-term success. Follow these nine steps and you'll be a pressure washing pro in no time flat.

You can also watch our "How to Start a Pressure Washing Business" video series to get advice from experts in action:

How to Start a Pressure Washing Business

Learn how to pressure wash

Pressure washing might seem easy enough, but you'll be working with high water pressure that can do serious (and expensive) damage. That's why you need to learn how to do the job right.

Rent a pressure washer or borrow a power washer from a neighbor. Then use it to remove dirt and grime from different types of durable surfaces, like driveways and vinyl siding.

Start in your own backyard, just in case you make a mistake. Find the best and fastest way of cleaning a particular surface without damaging it—or any items nearby, like plants or windows.

When you're feeling more confident, ask a friend or family member for a little extra practice on their property. You can also watch power washing tutorials or work for another pressure washing business to refine your technique.

Learning how to pressure wash will also tell you if you enjoy the job. If you don't, it's better to know right away—not after you've already bought pressure washing equipment.

Write a business plan

Creating a business plan helps you figure out how your business will operate. Some banks and lenders want to see business plans before they'll provide any funding.

Your pressure washing business plan should include:

- Cover page with your business name and the date

- Table of contents listing the different sections of the business plan

- Executive summary as a recap of the full document

- Business overview describing your pressure wash business and explaining what services you'll provide to which customers

- Services list showing which pressure washing services you'll provide to customers

- Pricing strategy with rates for each of your services
- Market analysis showing what area you'll serve and what customer demographics are there
- Competitive analysis of other local pressure washing businesses
- Marketing plan for reaching ideal customers and winning new work
- Employee planning with any roles you'll need and a hiring timeline
- Financial projections and cash flow strategy for your first year of business, including income, expenses, and salary

Even if you don't need a pressure washing business plan for a loan, it's still a good idea to make one. It'll help with long-term business planning and help you grow over the next several months and years.

You can find a more complete guide to writing a business plan from the Small Business Administration.

How much does it cost to start a pressure washing business?

Plan to spend around $1,975-4,900+ (USD) to start your pressure washing business. Here's what you'll need:

- Business license and registration ($75-400)

- Business insurance ($700-1,200+)

- Pressure washing software ($400)

- Branded uniform, waterproof boots, and safety gear ($50-150+)

- Pressure washing equipment ($600-2,600+)

- DIY website and business cards ($150)

If you need to buy a truck to transport yourself and your equipment to job sites, expect to spend an additional $10,000-30,000+. Factor in fuel, registration, and vehicle insurance, too.

You can get the startup funds you need through a personal or business loan, business credit card, government funding, business financing, or even a small business grant.

Get your free pressure washing estimate template

Create professional, branded estimates that wow your customers and win more jobs.

Identify your ideal customers

When you're just getting started, you might think it's good business practice to accept any job, anywhere. But that's how you end up with difficult customers who cause problems and cut into your profits.

Figure out who your perfect potential customer is and who would be the right fit for your power wash business. Put together an ideal customer profile that describes factors like:

- Market (residential, commercial, or industrial)
- Demographic (age, income, family status)
- Geographic location (neighborhood, town/city)
- Customer priorities (speed, price, quality)

Planning your pressure washing business with your ideal client profile in mind will help you keep customers happy, earn positive reviews, and get repeat customers.

FREE TOOL: Impress customers with our pressure washing receipt template

Invest in pressure washing equipment

It's time to go shopping head over to your local hardware store with this pressure washing equipment list and get the tools you need:

- Pressure washer
- Pressure washer pump
- Surface cleaner
- Water hoses
- Ladder
- Nozzles
- Telescoping wand
- Downstream injector
- Hose reel

- Water tank (for stronger equipment with greater water needs)
- Cleaning chemicals
- Heavy-duty extension cord (for electric pressure washers)

If you're starting a power washing business with a smaller rig, get a truck or a van for getting to job sites. You may also want a trailer if you have several large items to transport.

Pro Tip: Add your logo, phone number, and website to the side of your truck. That way it's doing double duty as a marketing channel for your pressure washing service.

What kind of pressure washer should I buy?

There are several different factors that determine the type of pressure washer you should buy:

- Power Source: Pressure washers can be powered by gas or electricity. If you buy a gas-powered machine, include fuel costs in your pressure washing pricing. If you buy electric, you'll need to either bring a generator or ask your clients to supply energy.
- Pressure: You can buy a light, medium, heavy-duty, or commercial pressure

washer. These offer different amounts of pressure for different types of jobs. The higher the pressure, the more grime the machine can handle.

- Temperature: If you know you'll be dealing with heavy-duty messes or commercial jobs, you might want to look at a power washer. It uses a combination of pressure and hot water to lift dirt away, while a standard pressure washer uses unheated water.

- Price: You might have room in your equipment budget for a brand-new, high-end machine—but it's also okay if you don't. You can always rent or lease a machine, or get a used one until you can afford something better.

Whatever you decide to buy, make sure it'll help you work faster, fit more jobs into your day, and make more money.

Decide which services to offer

There are different services you can offer as a pressure or power washing company. It all depends on whether you've decided to serve residential, commercial, or industrial customers.

Residential pressure washing services could include these types of exterior cleaning:

- Sidewalk and driveway cleaning

- Roof and gutter cleaning

- Window cleaning

- Siding, fence, and concrete cleaning

- Decks and patios

- Outdoor furniture and garbage bins

- Vehicle cleaning

Your industrial or commercial pressure washing service could include any of the above, as well as:

- Grease trap cleaning

- Graffiti removal

- Heavy machinery cleaning

- Commercial vehicle washing

- Post-construction cleaning

- Road and street sign cleaning

Limit the services you offer and focus on the ones you're best at. This will help narrow down your equipment list, reduce upfront costs, and boost your reputation faster.

Pro Tip: Different types of clients have different pressure washing needs. Make sure your equipment is right for each job—you don't want to shatter a window or tear away shingles on a customer's house with an industrial washer.

Make invoices easily and get paid faster

Use free pressure washing invoice generator to build a clean, professional invoice in just a few clicks.

Price your pressure washing services

Get your pricing in place before you start looking for work. Depending on the scope, surface area, and geographic location, the average pressure washing price for a job is:

- House washing: $89-633
- Driveway pressure washing: $66-348
- Window washing: $56-567
- Deck washing: $48-827
- Fence washing: $41-352

Here's how to price pressure washing jobs:

- Research competitor pricing to see what other local pressure washers are charging for their services. Figure out why they charge what they do.

- Estimate labor costs by multiplying your hourly wage by the number of hours you think it'll take to complete the job.

- Calculate monthly overhead expenses, then divide by the number of hours you work every month to get your hourly overhead.

- Estimate material costs like cleaning chemicals, fuel, or other supplies you'll bring to the job. Add a markup for the time and effort it took to buy those materials.

- Account for profit margin, which is the amount of income your business gets to keep after all job expenses. Aim for 10-20% of the overall project value.

- Factor in taxes, including income and sales tax, and multiply your subtotal by that percentage.
- Add it all up and you'll see how much to charge for a pressure wash. Based on that, you can charge customers the hourly rate, or adapt that amount to provide fixed fee or square footage pricing.

Register your pressure washing business

Before you can start running your pressure washing or power washer business, you need to register and license it. Here's how:

- Choose a pressure washing business name that describes who you are and what services you provide. The name should be memorable and unique in your area. Next, use that name to create a logo with an online tool like Looka.

- Pick a business structure—in the U.S., that's usually a sole proprietor, partnership, or limited liability company (LLC), or limited liability partnership (LLP). There are more entity options in other countries. You can also choose to incorporate your business.

- Register your business through your local registry. If you're in the U.S., you'll pay a fee, trademark your name, and register your domain name. (Here's how to register in Canada, the UK, or Australia.) Requirements vary depending on where you live, so get more information from the business registration division in your area.

- Get a business permit or license so you can legally work in your area. Talk to your local Chamber of Commerce to see what type of license you need and apply for it. It's important that you understand licensing requirements in your area—working without a license can earn a hefty fine or even lead to your business closing.

- Open a business bank account for tracking expenses and payments. This will keep your personal funds separate from business funds. Speak with the business services team at your bank to get started.

- Apply for an EIN if you plan to hire soon or work with a partner. An employer identification number will be a big help when you're filing taxes with the Internal Revenue Service.

- Get small business insurance to protect your business in case of any accidents or issues. Purchase a business owner's policy that includes general liability, commercial property, and business income insurance.

You can also get policies to cover you in case of other unexpected problems.

Get customers for your pressure washing business

Marketing your pressure washing company will help you bring in new clients, finish jobs, and get paid. Try these ideas for reaching potential customers and turning them into pressure washing leads:

- Word of mouth is the most effective marketing channel for pressure washing businesses. Encourage customers to talk about your services by setting up a referral program and asking for online reviews.

- Create social media profiles on Facebook, Twitter, or Instagram to help your pressure washing business get noticed in your community. Choose the platforms where your ideal customers spend time online, then post content regularly and engage with your followers.

- Build a website where potential customers can learn about your pressure washing services, see before-and-after photos of finished jobs, and book services online.

- List your business on online directories where potential customers look for pressure washers, like Google Business, Yelp for Business, and Bing Places.

- Network with other entrepreneurs and reach new potential customers by joining your local business association, taking part in pressure washing associations and groups, supporting community events, and promoting your business whenever you can.

- Print pressure washing flyers and hand them out door-to-door in the neighborhoods where you'd like to work. You can also leave behind yard signs after you complete each job, if your customers allow it.

- Buy business cards, branded uniforms, and a vehicle wrap. This reinforces your business branding while you're on the job and makes your business look polished and professional. You can also brand your quotes, invoices, emails, and other materials.

- Pressure washing marketing costs will depend on which platforms you choose. For example, you can create a website and business cards for $150, or spend $2,000 on a billboard.

The best way to use your budget is to reach potential customers in the places where they spend time. Later, you can create a digital marketing strategy using tactics like Google ads and Facebook ads.

Grow your pressure washing business

You need to stay one step ahead to build a successful pressure washing business. Think about how you'll keep your clients satisfied, earn a solid reputation, and grow your company over time.

Here are some ideas to get you started:

- Hire your first employee to help you with day-to-day work, allowing you to focus more on growing the business. Get started with our pressure washer job description.
- Enter new markets to reach new clients, or offer new services to earn more from your current clients.

- Squeeze more jobs into each day with more efficient routing and keep an eye on your team's progress with GPS tracking.

- Offer a client hub where your customers can approve estimates, book appointments, and pay invoices.

- After finishing a job, send a customer service follow-up email along with an opportunity to schedule the next appointment.

- Automate client emails to help you stay in touch during quoting, invoicing, and payment, without any extra effort.

- That's enough planning. Now that you know how to start a power washing business, it's time to get to work! You're ready to start and grow a successful business—no pressure.

3.1 9 Types of Equipment Needed to Start a Pressure Washing Business

If you have decided to start a power washing business, that's exciting news. With low start-up costs and high-profit margins, a pressure washing business is a great side hustle that can very well grow into a full-time career.

There are many different types of equipment you will need to start your power washing business. This book will list the basic equipment you'll need for your pressure washing business. If you don't have the budget to cover the high cost of certain equipment, you can consider renting them.

Here's the list of equipment needed to start your power washing business.

Trailer, van, or truck

You'll need a trailer, van, or truck to transport your tools and machines. Considering your budget, you can either choose to buy or rent it. It's recommended to buy a closed truck/van as it provides better protection from loss, damage, and theft. You can also use your vehicle as an effective advertising tool. Make sure the vehicle can take the heavy load of your power washing tools and equipment.

High-pressure washers

You'll need a power washer that provides a force of 3,000 PSI or more. The higher the pressure, the better and faster is the cleaning. If you want to use a lower pressure on certain surfaces, you can always attach a larger spray tip to it.

Electric motor or a gas engine

You'll need this motor to generate pressure or to heat water for various cleaning operations. When buying an electric motor or gas engine, make sure you stick to the ones that are known for reliability and consistency.

Hot water units

You'll need a hot water unit to give you the hot water you need to clean surfaces efficiently. This unit must be at least 18 HP with V-twin motors.

High- and low-pressure water hoses

You'll need these hoses to regulate the pressure depending on the surfaces you are working on. A hose of 50 feet in length with portable carrying cases is ideal. You might have to consider different hoses for using hot and cold water and the ones designed to carry chemicals.

Nozzles

You'll need a turbocharged nozzle that can be used on concrete and other hard substances.

X-jet

You'll need an X-jet to wash houses, buildings, and other structures using soap and chemicals. You can use this tool with or without hoses or lances. An X-jet is also useful for sterilizing chemicals when cleaning livestock/poultry barns and pens or spraying insecticides.

Sewer jetters

You'll need a sewer jetter to flush sewers. So make sure the sewer jetters you buy are powerful, exerting pressures of 2,500 PSI to 4,000 PSI that can clear all the debris. Sewer jetters are also effective in removing mineral residue or corrosion.

Pressure washer gun assembly

You'll need a pressure wash gun assembly that has a gun, a hose connector, and a mosmatic swivel. All these work together to save time and effort on the cleaning job.

3.2 ADVANTAGES OF USING HIGH-QUALITY EqUIPMENT FOR PRESSURE CLEANING

When purchasing or hiring pressure washing equipment, make sure you get the highest quality equipment and tools available.

In the initial stages of your power washing business, it's important that you build goodwill to earn repeat business and referrals. High-quality equipment helps you do a thorough cleaning job, earning the loyalty of your customers.

High-quality equipment is studier and lasts longer.

Using high-grade, expensive equipment helps you build credibility in the mind of the client, who will appreciate the quality of service you are providing.

Pressure cleaning is a labor-intensive business. When you use the right, high-quality tools and equipment, the time and labor you spend on each job are reduced.

High-quality equipment usually has a written warranty. This helps you save costs on repair.

3.3 What Do You Need to Pressure Wash a Driveway?

Before we discuss how to pressure wash a concrete driveway or how to pressure wash a brick driveway, you need to gather all the supplies needed for this cleaning method. Having the right equipment and products is crucial if you want to properly pressure wash a driveway. Here's what you need:

Pressure Washer

You need a high-quality pressure washer that can deliver about 3,000 pounds per square inch (PSI). The higher the PSI, the faster and more effectively you can clean your driveway.

Cleaning Agents

While pressurized water can be enough to clean your driveway, cleaning agents such as soap or detergent help loosen up all the dirt, grime, and grease. They're also great for targeting stubborn stains. Choose a cleaning agent that is specifically made for your driveway pressure washer.

Pressure Washer Hose

If a pressure washer hose is out of the budget, you can instead use a garden hose. Preferably, the hose should be 50 feet long to provide you with a wide range of motion.

Broom or Stiff Brush

You also need a broom or a long-handled brush to scrub away the dirt and grime from your driveway. Make sure to use one that has stiff bristles to prevent splash-backs and effectively clean your surface.

Safety Gear

Pressure washing driveways can be dangerous. The high-pressure water can injure your eyes, hands, and feet. Make sure to wear a long-sleeve shirt, long pants, and rubber-soled shoes, as well as safety goggles, gloves, and hearing protection.

Plastic Sheets or Garbage Bags

Plastic sheets or garbage bags are used to protect other areas of your home while pressure washing the driveway.

Painter's Tape

A painter's tape will secure your plastic sheets so that water doesn't seep into other areas of your home.

3.4 7 Easy Steps to Pressure Wash a Driveway

If you want to learn how to pressure wash a driveway, follow these 7 easy steps:

Clear the Surface

The first step is to prepare your driveway and surrounding areas for pressure washing. Clear away debris and items, and make sure to sweep away all excess dirt from the surface.

Protect Doors and Windows

Door and windows of a house protected by metal blinds | pressure wash your drivewayDoors, windows, and other sensitive areas can become damaged as you pressure wash a driveway. Due to the pressure of the water, small rocks, debris, and other contaminants can be flung into the air and sent to different areas of your property.

Avoid this by covering windows, doors, and other sensitive areas with plastic sheets or garbage bags. Many beginners forget about this important precaution, but this is the best way to minimize any risk or damage as you pressure wash your driveway. Use painter's tape to secure the sheets and prevent water from seeping into your home.

Assemble Pressure Washer

There isn't a single standard for pressure washers, so make sure to read your machine's manual. It's important to understand the power settings and other features of your pressure washer. If assembled or used incorrectly, the pressure washer could harm the surface of your driveway.

Wear Safety Gear

Before starting the cleaning process, make sure that you are properly dressed and have the appropriate safety gear for pressure washing a driveway.

Apply Cleaning Agent

Apply your chosen cleaning agent to the driveway. This will help loosen up dirt, grime, and stains on the surface. If your pressure washer doesn't have a brush attachment, use a broom to scrub the surface.

Pressure Wash Your Driveway

Outdoor floor Worker cleaning driveway with a pressure water jet | pressure wash drivewayNow that everything has been prepared, it's time to pressure wash your driveway. Hold down the spray handle, and move side to side across the surface of your driveway. Try to overlap each movement by about half a foot. Remember that proper techniques will vary depending on your pressure washer. When dealing with tough stains, you may have to hold your pressure washer closer to the surface.

Rinse the Surface

Rinse your driveway to wash away leftover soap or detergent as well as remaining dirt and grime. Then, allow the surface to dry. You can apply a sealant to protect your driveway from future stains.

3.5 Pressure Washing Driveway Tips to Remember

It may seem easy to pressure wash driveways by yourself but to do it correctly, you need skill and experience. As a beginner, you're likely not familiar with all the intricacies involved with pressure washing a driveway. Not only can you damage your driveway, but you can also cause serious harm or injury. Here are some pressure washing driveway tips to keep in mind.

Start with a low PSI.

Pressure gauge showing zero psi | pressure washing drivewayYou may be surprised at the power of pressure washers when it comes to spraying water. If you start out with a high PSI, you can easily lose control of the pressure washer. The spray is strong enough to cause wounds or damage property. Though a low PSI will be less effective in cleaning your driveway, this will give you enough time to adjust to the pressure washer.

Never point the pressure washer at yourself or at other people.

Always point the pressure washer wand downward. If you are not operating the pressure washer, make sure the wand is secure. A small accident or slip can turn on the machine and cause serious damage.

Do not use a gasoline-powered pressure washer in enclosed spaces.

Gasoline-powered pressure washers emit carbon monoxide, so it should only be used in well-ventilated areas. Carbon monoxide poisoning can be fatal in a matter of minutes.

Keep the power cord and/or extension cord far away from water.

If you have to use a power cord or an extension cord, make sure it's as far away from the driveway as possible. Avoid placing it in areas where water runoff can reach. If possible, use a heavy-duty extension cord that is properly grounded.

If you are unsure, don't hesitate to contact a professional pressure washing service.

While going the DIY route might seem like a more economical choice, there are a lot of risks involved in pressure washing a driveway. If you don't think you will be able to do this correctly, it might be better to use a professional pressure washing service.

3.6 REASONS TO CONSIDER PROFESSIONAL PRESSURE WASHING

Here are some great reasons for professional driveway pressure washing:

Experience and Expertise

A professional pressure washing company will know how to effectively clean your driveway as well as other parts of your house.

Professional-Grade Equipment

They have high-quality pressure washers, environment-friendly cleaning products, and other tools needed to clean your driveway. To even come close to what the professionals are using, you will have to spend a lot of money.

No Damage or Injury

Professional pressure washers won't cause any damage to your property or injure anyone while cleaning your driveway. Even if they make mistakes, they are fully insured and can compensate you for damages.

Saves Time and Energy

Pressure washing a driveway is very time-consuming. If you're a beginner, it's possible that you may not achieve the results you want on the first try. Thus, you'll have to repeat the whole process. Have a professional crew take care of your driveway so you can enjoy your hard-earned weekend.

Cost-Effective in the Long Run

Given all the risks of DIY pressure washing, professional pressure washing might be more cost-effective in the long run. If you end up damaging your driveway, doors, or windows, you'll end up having to spend more on repairs.

3.7 Pressure Wash a Driveway Without Any Stress

It's normal for your driveway to have some wear and tear. However, if you want to extend its life, regular maintenance is crucial. Pressure washing allows you to blast away all the dirt, grime, and stains on the surface. If you're a beginner looking to pressure wash a driveway, there's no need to fret. As long as you follow this beginner's guide, you'll be able to clean your driveway without any stress. If you're hesitant, though, don't hesitate to give us a call. We can restore your driveway and have it look almost new.

3.8 How to Pressure Wash a Deck or Patio

Patios and decks are generally made of wood or cement and can usually be cleaned using the same techniques—hand or pressure washing. Washh recommends that you go with the pressure washing method because it is quicker and easier. For tougher stains, you may need to resort to calling professionals who know how to power wash a deck with just the right nozzle and temperature settings.

When it comes to your deck or patio investment, it pays to get the job done by pros.

4 PRESSURE WASHING SAFETY PROTOCOLS

When you conduct the pressure washing method, make sure that you comply with the following safety protocols:

- To ensure that your eyes are protected, wear safety goggles. When you pressure wash, small pieces of debris like pebbles and sticks can fly into the air and hit you in sensitive areas, like the eyes. Keep your eyes safe, and wear goggles as a preventative measure.

- Safeguard your home by placing plastic sheeting or trash bags over sensitive areas of your home, such as windows or doors. In addition to covering your eyes, you need to protect your home from damage, especially if it is near your deck or patio.

- Keep your pressure washer at an appropriate pressure level. If your washer has too much pressure, it can potentially damage your surfaces—you certainly don't want to crack or dent your patio or deck surface. For the best results, contact a professional. They will get the job done right, without damaging your surfaces.

4.1 5 STEPS TO PRESSURE WASH A DECK OR PATIO

To safely and successfully pressure wash your patio and deck, follow these five recommended steps:

Plan and Be Prepared

Make sure that you plan when you decide to tackle this project. You don't want to go into the task unprepared. It is important to know what you are getting yourself into, and that you follow all recommended safety precautions. If you are inexperienced or unprepared for the pressure washing task, have a professional crew get the job done for you.

For wooden decks, plan to have the equipment you need to pressure wash a deck safely. Most experts recommend having a pressure washer nozzle with a rotating tip. A nozzle with a wide fan tip is also a good alternative.

Pressure washing can impart enough force to etch even brick, so pick just the right pressure for your wooden deck. The same goes for your brick and concrete patio, too. Use the lowest possible pressure that still gets the job done. If possible, test your pressure washing settings on an area that people won't see.

Also, consider if a power wash is the better option for your deck or patio. Power wash uses hot water to lift stains, so you don't need as much detergent. Do note that not all surfaces are safe to power wash.

Move Furniture and Other Items

Before you start pressure washing your patio or deck, you need to move all furniture and items, such as chairs, tables, fire pits, etc. out of the way. This allows you space and access to properly wash your surfaces. Plus, pressure washers can be damaging to patio and deck furniture, so make sure to take the necessary precautions to take care of your belongings by moving them far from the areas you plan on washing.

Sweep Away All Debris

Your patio and deck are exposed to mother nature year-round—snow, rain, sleet, wind, you name it. Over time, sticks, leaves, debris, and contaminants will build upon your surfaces. Before pressure washing, make sure you clear all debris off your surfaces. This allows you the proper space and access to execute a quality wash.

Start Pressure Washing or Power Washing

Once you sweep away all debris and move all furniture, it is time to execute the pressure washing. When you pressure wash you will want to use a cleaner, especially if you are cleaning surfaces with tough-to-reach stains. Remember that it is important to focus on removing dirt and grime from the grains and cracks of your surface— contaminants will build up and degrade these areas over time if you don't follow proper washing methods.

When pressure washing wooden patios, remember to spray along the grain, not across it. Doing so decreases the chance that the water jet can cause splinters.

Carefully Rinse All Soap and Detergent Residue

Pressure washing wooden deck close up | how to power wash a deckAfter you finish your pressure washing, make sure to rinse your surfaces. It's very important to rinse after pressure washing with soap. Any soap residue left on your patio or deck will dry and become sticky, and attract more dirt and grime. This will reverse the results of your pressure washing efforts, so make sure to thoroughly rinse away all soap from the surfaces. Once you complete this step, let the deck or patio dry for a while.

5 CONCLUSION

Power washers are an efficient way to clean a variety of surfaces, from cars and boats to pressure-washing driveways and decks. However, they can be dangerous if not used properly, so it's essential to follow some basic safety guidelines.

Choose the right power washer: There are different types of pressure washers, with varying levels of pressure and flow rate. Choose one that's suitable for the task at hand, based on the size and type of surface you're cleaning.

Prepare the area: Remove any debris or obstacles from the area you're planning to clean. Cover any delicate plants or objects that could be damaged by the pressure washer.

Connect the power washer: Follow the manufacturer's instructions to connect the hoses and attachments. Make sure all connections are secure and the machine is properly grounded.

Turn on the machine: Start the pressure washer by following the manufacturer's instructions. Most machines have an on/off switch and a throttle or pressure adjustment control.

Test the pressure: Before you start cleaning, test the power washer on a small, inconspicuous area of the surface to be cleaned. This will help you determine the right pressure and distance to hold the wand from the surface to avoid damaging it.

Clean the surface: Using the pressure washer wand, work in a sweeping motion from side to side, keeping the nozzle about 6-8 inches away from the surface. Use a detergent if needed, following the manufacturer's instructions. Rinse thoroughly, and repeat if necessary.

Turn off the machine: Once you've finished cleaning, turn off the power washer and disconnect the hoses. Store the machine in a dry,

cool place.

www.ingramcontent.com/pod-product-compliance
Lightning Source LLC
Chambersburg PA
CBHW072330290526
45794CB00002B/812